BURMESE PYTHONS

WILLOW CLARK

PowerKiDS
press™

New York

Published in 2013 by The Rosen Publishing Group, Inc.
29 East 21st Street, New York, NY 10010

Copyright © 2013 by The Rosen Publishing Group, Inc.

All rights reserved. No part of this book may be reproduced in any form without permission in writing from the publisher, except by a reviewer.

First Edition

Editor: Joanne Randolph
Book Design: Ashley Drago

Photo Credits: Cover © www.iStockphoto.com/Paul Tessier; pp. 4, 7 (bottom), 8, 19 (right), 20 Heiko Kiera/Shutterstock.com; p. 5 Comstock/Thinkstock.com; p. 7 (top) Joe McDonald/Visuals Unlimited/Getty Images; p. 9 © H. Schmidbauer/Age Fotostock; p. 10 Photo Researchers/Getty Images; p. 11 New York Daily News Archive/Contributor/Getty Images; p. 13 James H. Robinson/Photo Researchers/Getty Images; p. 14 Gabriel Bouys/AFP Creative/Getty Images; pp. 15, 16 John Mitchell/Photo Researchers/Getty Images; p. 17 E. R. Degginger/Photo Researchers/Getty Images; p. 18 Jupiter Images/Photos.com/Thinkstock; p. 19 (left) Matt Hart/Shutterstock.com; p. 21 Jim Merli/Visuals Unlimited/Getty Images; p. 22 Simon D. Pollard/Photo Researchers/Getty Images.

Library of Congress Cataloging-in-Publication Data

Clark, Willow.
Burmese pythons / by Willow Clark. — 1st ed.
p. cm. — (The animals of Asia)
Includes index.
ISBN 978-1-4488-7418-7 (library binding) — ISBN 978-1-4488-7491-0 (pbk.) —
ISBN 978-1-4488-7565-8 (6-pack)
1. Burmese python—Juvenile literature. I. Title.
QL666.O63C53 2013
597.96′78—dc23

2012004244

Manufactured in China

CPSIA Compliance Information: Batch #WKTS12PK: For Further Information contact Rosen Publishing, New York, New York at 1-800-237-9932

CONTENTS

HELLO, PYTHON!

The Burmese python is one of the world's largest snakes. This snake is one of two **subspecies** of the Indian python. A subspecies is a smaller group within a **species**. The Burmese

Burmese pythons like to climb trees.

python lives in South Asia and Southeast Asia. These snakes are known for their beautifully patterned skin, which makes them popular as pets.

Like other pythons, the Burmese python is a **constrictor**. That means that instead of killing **prey** with a **venomous** bite, pythons kill their prey by squeezing it.

◄ *Many people keep Burmese pythons as pets. Pet Burmese pythons often have lighter coloring than those in the wild.*

WHERE IN THE WORLD?

Burmese pythons get their name from Burma, one of the countries to which they are native. Today this country is called Myanmar. Burmese pythons are also found in Thailand, Malaysia, Indonesia, and southern China.

This map shows where in the world wild Burmese pythons live.
▼

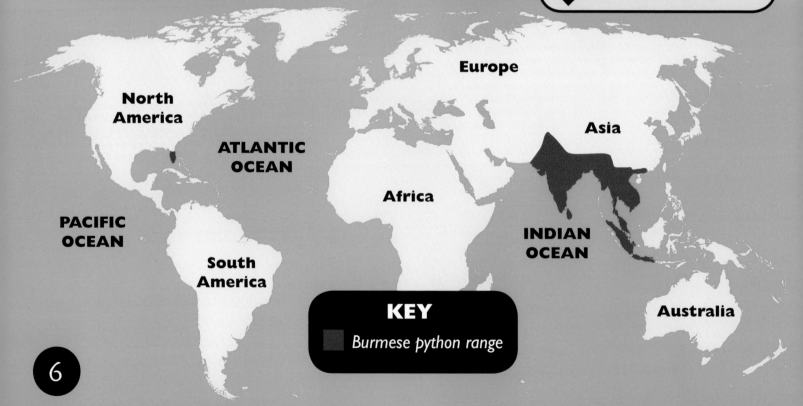

Europe

North America

Asia

ATLANTIC OCEAN

Africa

PACIFIC OCEAN

INDIAN OCEAN

South America

Australia

KEY

Burmese python range

Top: There are also Burmese pythons in Florida's Everglades. These snakes do not belong there. Pet owners who no longer wanted their snakes put them there. Bottom: This Burmese python rests on a log by the water in Asia.

Across its range, the Burmese python lives mostly in rain forests. It can live in other kinds of habitats if they are near water, though. Burmese pythons are also found in grasslands and swamps.

IN THE TREES AND ON THE GROUND

Young Burmese pythons spend a lot of time in trees. As they grow and get heavier, tree climbing becomes harder and adults spend most of their time on the ground. Burmese pythons are also great swimmers. They can stay underwater for up to 30 minutes at a time!

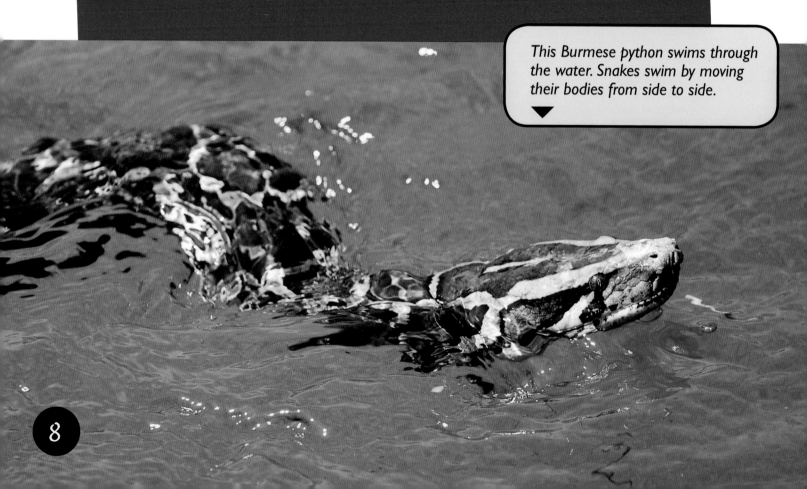

This Burmese python swims through the water. Snakes swim by moving their bodies from side to side.

▼

A *Burmese python may wrap its body around a tree branch to rest, as this one has done.*

Throughout much of the Burmese python's range, the climate is warm year-round. In the northern parts of its range, the weather cools between October and February, though. During this time, Burmese pythons will **brumate** in a hollow tree, under rocks, or in a hole in the ground.

A REALLY BIG SNAKE

Burmese pythons are one of the world's biggest snakes. They can grow to be up to 23 feet (7 m) long and weigh up to 200 pounds (90 kg). A full-grown snake might be as thick as a telephone pole at its widest point!

Female Burmese pythons are larger than males. It takes these snakes several years to reach full size. ▼

This five-year-old Burmese python is showing off its huge size to a group of fifth-grade students at the American Museum of Natural History, in New York City.

Due to their size, Burmese pythons find it easiest to move forward in a straight line. They use their ribs for support and use their belly scales to push themselves forward. This is not a very fast way to move. Burmese pythons can move only about 1 mile per hour (2 km/h).

SNAKE SCALES

Like other snakes, Burmese pythons are **reptiles**. Reptiles are cold-blooded animals that breathe air and have skin that is covered in scales. A cold-blooded animal is one that has a body temperature that is close to the temperature of its surroundings. This is why you sometimes see a snake sunning itself to warm up.

Burmese pythons have unevenly shaped, dark spots with lighter bands between them. ▶

Burmese pythons may be tan, yellowish brown, or gray. They have patterns of markings that run the length of their bodies. Pet snakes are sometimes bred to be lighter than snakes in the wild. You might see yellow or even white Burmese pythons in a pet store.

HUNTING FOR FOOD

When you see a snake like the Burmese python flicking its tongue in and out of its mouth, it is smelling the air. A snake's sense of smell is its strongest sense. It uses this sense to hunt for prey. Smells are carried by the tongue to a special organ in the roof of the snake's mouth. This special body part is called the **Jacobson's organ**.

◀ Here a python is smelling its surroundings. Pythons have poor eyesight, so they count on their sense of smell.

The Jacobson's organ is on the roof of the Burmese python's mouth, which you see here. Pythons can open their mouths really wide. This lets them swallow large animals.

Burmese pythons also have heat-sensing pits along their jawlines. These pits let the snake sense the body heat of nearby animals. Jacobson's organs and heat-sensing pits help Burmese pythons find prey in thick foliage and even in the dark.

A TIGHT SQUEEZE

The Burmese python is an ambush hunter. That means these snakes do not chase prey but catch it by surprise. Constrictors like the Burmese python do not have fangs, as do venomous snakes. Instead of fangs, pythons have teeth that curve

This Burmese python is constricting a rodent. Once the animal dies, the snake can swallow the prey whole. ▼

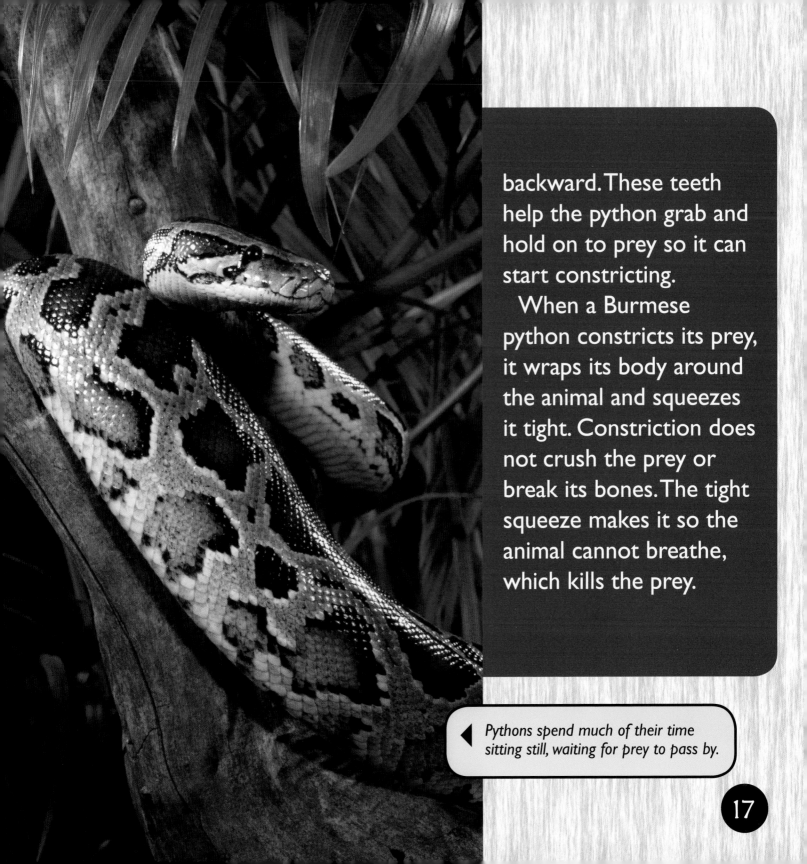

backward. These teeth help the python grab and hold on to prey so it can start constricting.

When a Burmese python constricts its prey, it wraps its body around the animal and squeezes it tight. Constriction does not crush the prey or break its bones. The tight squeeze makes it so the animal cannot breathe, which kills the prey.

Pythons spend much of their time sitting still, waiting for prey to pass by.

WHAT'S FOR LUNCH?

Burmese pythons are **carnivores**. That means that they eat other animals. Their diet is made up mostly of small **mammals** and birds. They do not eat every day, so these snakes make every meal count!

Burmese pythons usually consume their prey headfirst.

Burmese pythons will eat jungle fowl or even domesticated chickens.

Burmese pythons eat rodents, such as rats and mice. They have also been known to eat larger prey, such as deer and alligators.

After it catches its prey, the Burmese python unhinges its jaw and begins to swallow the animal whole. This allows it to swallow prey that is several times larger than its head! Next, the python's strong body muscles pull the food down the snake's throat and into its stomach. It will spend the next few days sunning itself and digesting its meal.

BABY PYTHONS

Burmese pythons are ready to **mate** when they are 7 to 9 feet (2–3 m) long. This size is generally reached by the snake between the ages of four and five.

Once the baby pythons hatch, they face many dangers. Baby pythons are eaten by many kinds of birds and even other snakes. ▼

The mother snake will not even leave her eggs to eat during the two months it takes them to hatch.

After mating, the female lays around 35 eggs. She then coils around her eggs and stays with them until they hatch about two months later. If the temperature gets chilly, the mother can warm up her eggs by using her muscles to make shivering movements around the eggs. The mother leaves once the baby pythons hatch, and they must take care of themselves.

BURMESE PYTHONS IN TROUBLE

The Burmese python is a widespread species, but its numbers are falling. It could become **endangered**. One reason that Burmese pythons are in trouble is habitat loss.

> *As people move farther into places that were once wild, there are fewer places for wild animals like the Burmese python to live.* ▶

People hunt Burmese pythons for their skin and their meat, and the snake is also a popular exotic pet. Some countries now have laws that protect these big snakes so that they will be around for years to come.

GLOSSARY

BRUMATE (BROO-mayt) To stop body processes for a period of time. Brumation is like hibernation in mammals.

CARNIVORES (KAHR-neh-vorz) Animals that eat only other animals.

CONSTRICTOR (kun-STRIKT-ur) A snake that kills by wrapping its body around its prey and squeezing.

ENDANGERED (in-DAYN-jerd) In danger of no longer living.

JACOBSON'S ORGAN (JAY-kub-sunz OR-gun) A kind of sensory organ that helps lizards' and snakes' sense of smell and taste.

MAMMALS (MA-mulz) Warm-blooded animals that have backbones and hair, breathe air, and feed milk to their young.

MATE (MAYT) To come together to make babies.

PREY (PRAY) An animal that is hunted by another animal for food.

REPTILES (REP-tylz) Cold-blooded animals with thin, dry pieces of skin called scales.

SPECIES (SPEE-sheez) One kind of living thing. All people are one species.

SUBSPECIES (SUB-spee-sheez) Different kinds of the same animal.

VENOMOUS (VEH-nuh-mis) Having matter that can cause pain or death.

INDEX

WEBSITES

Due to the changing nature of Internet links, PowerKids Press has developed an online list of websites related to the subject of this book. This site is updated regularly. Please use this link to access the list: www.powerkidslinks.com/aoa/pyth/